DIARY OF A CRUSH

Cover art from Lulu.com

All of the material contained in this book is the original work of the author.

Published 2009

Lulu Press
860 Aviation Parkway
Morrisville, NC 27560

Printed in the United States of America

ISBN: 978-0-557-20090-0

Books by Lena Kovadlo

Pieces of Me
Soundtrack of My Life: Volume 1
Soundtrack of My Life: Volume 2
Diary of a Crush

I'd like to thank James L. Finley - also a published author with his debut poetry book Wandering Wounds - for taking the time to help me proofread and edit this book. Your tremendous help is greatly appreciated and I am thrilled that you took part in bringing this book to life.

I dedicate this book to all those who have ever been in love, all those who have yet to experience its ups and downs, and all those who have found themselves having a crush on that special someone.

Greetings to all you love birds out there. My name is LoveBug, and I am here to spread the different seeds of love all around. I sit here under a shady tree in the park and let my pen leave its mark on the empty pages of my diary. I pour out my soul about crushes, guys, relationships, love, heartbreak, and more. So sit back and get ready to dive into the garden of love that is Diary of a Crush.

TABLE OF CONTENTS:

TABLE OF CONTENTS:

TABLE OF CONTENTS:

SECTION I
VERSES OF A CRUSH

BEING WITHOUT YOU

October 22, 2007

As minutes slowly drag the time,
My heart is empty with longing,
Yearning for your words,
For your voice,
For your closeness,
And perhaps for your touch.

Being without your presence,
In whatever way possible,
Is pure torture,
Enveloping me in sorrow,
And bringing with it,
Endless salty tears,
That cloud my beautiful face.

You are always on my mind,
And there in my beating heart,
That bursts with love,
And craves for your soul.

Without you I am drowning,
And only you can save me,
So wherever you are,
Come and rescue me away.
Let me know of your existence,
And your presence in mine,
Otherwise, I might not see tomorrow.

TWO ANGELS AND THE MAGIC OF LOVE

November 22, 2007

As I stand here in the shower,
The water trickling down my slender frame,
I feel the cool drops
Refreshing every inch of my naked flesh.

I feel your fingers gliding down my body,
Tingling me from head to toe.

I feel your lips brush against mine,
Ever so gently,
Locking with my own,
And never letting them part,
The kisses sending shivers down my spine.

I feel your warm embrace surround me,
With the love that burns from within.

I feel your presence right here in the shower,
As we melt away under the liquid drops,
You and I caught in this passionate moment,
Transporting us into a heavenly paradise,
Where time comes to a standstill,
And there is nothing but you and I,
Two angels caught in the magic of love,
That will never fade with time's passing,
And will only continue to flame and grow.

CHRISTMAS MIRACLE

December 17, 2007

You're my Christmas miracle,
You're my shining star,
Up there on my Christmas tree,
Stretching wide and far.

You're my snow angel,
That guards me through the day.
You're the beautiful snowflakes,
Falling down my face.

You're my Christmas present,
On a cold Christmas Eve.
When my birthday's here,
You're just what I need.

But you'll never be here,
Because you're miles away,
And I'll find myself blue
Unable to pass the day.

At least I'll feel your love,
You sent across the miles,
And that will bring the happiness,
And lots of widest smiles.

You're my Christmas miracle,
Of that I have no doubt,
Because you came into my life,
And turned it inside out.

You made me feel complete,
And filled my empty heart.
You made me feel so special,
Right from the very start.

And you're the perfect present,
Beneath the Christmas tree,
That I have ever gotten,
Or will receive you see.

The only thing that's better,
Is if you're by my side,
And when that finally happens,
You'll be forever mine.

So that's the Christmas miracle,
I'll wish with snow each year,
Until you're really in my arms,
To love and hold dear.

THE COLORS OF LOVE

January 10, 2008

My world was gray and cloudy
Until you came along.
Blue with lots of rainy days,
I was drowning in my song.

And when night crept up on me,
I felt alone and hollow.
I always craved for sunlight,
And wished it was tomorrow.

I never thought it possible,
That someday I would find,
Someone as sweet and caring,
Someone who'd blow my mind.

Then one fine day to my surprise,
You came and rescued me.
An angel sent here from above,
You've drowned my misery.

No longer is my world so blue,
Or gray, or black, or hollow.
It's filled with only brightest hues,
And colorful tomorrows.

Diary of a Crush

To me the grays are snowflakes,
That penetrate my soul.
And black is filled with magic stars,
As nightly dreams afloat.

There's burning reds of flaming love,
The warmth of orange sun.
There's the embrace of waterfalls,
Refreshing and so calm.

And there's the lightest blue in me,
When tears start to stream,
But these are drops of happiness,
For sorrow's not within.

There's every kind of color now,
But each is filled with love,
Thanks to the sweetest caring angel,
Sent to me from above.

SHATTERED HEART

January 19, 2008

You tore my heart
You shattered it
I loved you but
This love was tart
When you just left
Like I was gone
Did you expect
I'd just move on
I tried and tried
To get you out
Out of my life
Out of my head
It didn't work
My heart was dead
It took a while
For me to heal
To mend this heart
To live again
It seems the love
For you was gone
Who was I kidding
It's still strong
Cause from this dream
I had of you
All of these feelings
Flooded back
I love you so
I never stopped
Deep down inside
It always burned
And here I am

In love with you
        To find that you
Have vanished from
        My life for good
I'm in a brawl
        I'm happy cause
I love you so
        But I am torn
Cause you are gone
        And to my world
You'll not return
        Leaving me here
To fight this war
        Until I'm old
And gray and more
        Till it won't matter
Anymore

SO SPECIAL

January 25, 2008

Deep within my dancing heart,
Lives a love so strong and bright,
And it burns for you my sweet,
Every morning, day, and night.

You'll forever live in me,
Whether you are near or far,
And you'll always hold a place,
That's so special in my heart.

CLOSER TO YOU

February 9, 2008

Every letter, every call,
Brings you closer to my soul.
Yet you're still so far away,
And I miss you lots each day,
And I will until you're here
In my arms to hold dear.

LEFT WITH A BROKEN HEART

May 22, 2008

All was bliss,
And yes we met.
Three incredible days
I'll never forget.

But then things changed
And he started to vanish,
And that left me torn,
My heart was tarnished.

The first guy I loved
And thought was the one,
Left me in the dust
For someone else.

I wanted him around
And thought we'd be friends,
But he just ignored me
And that is the end.

It's like I don't exist,
It's like he doesn't care.
It hurts me so much
And that is not fair.

I think I've moved on,
Yet still feel the pain,
To know my undying love
For him was in vain.

HOOKED ON YOU

May 25, 2008

I am in heaven
Night and day.
I'm blessed that you
Have come my way.

You're on my mind,
In my embrace.
The widest smile
Won't leave my face.

You're my addiction.
You're my drug.
I'm hooked on you.
Can't get enough.

PIECES OF ME

May 28, 2008

These pieces of me will engrave on your heart,
To treasure forever and never to part.
The beauty and song of the words of my soul,
Will embrace you my angel in a passionate hold.
You will drown in bliss and in love burning bright.
Your days they will sparkle like snowflakes at night.
And the bond that has bloomed between you and me,
With our spirits entwined will never set free.

SWEETNESS THAT IS YOU

June 12, 2008

The sweet juices escape from you like flowing rivers,
Penetrating my soul and every bit of my flesh,
Caressing me with a thirst of hunger,
That only you can quench.
You make me sweat those juices,
And drown in the sweetness that is you.

BURIED

July 16, 2008 & July 17, 2008

I am buried inside
Your molecular love,
And up to the heavens
I am soaring above.

I am floating through space
To the magical stars,
And sip every morsel
Of the mystery of ours.

I am buried alive
Inside of your soul,
And there I will linger
And never let go.

Your passion, your fire,
They feed me the power,
And with it I battle
The sorrowful hour.

The days buried with time,
Now I wear the crown.
I am winning this fight,
No more reason to drown.

I will always be swimming
In nothing but bliss,
And the loneliest hour
Will just be dismissed.

Because you are here
And never to part.
You keep the flame burning
Inside of my heart.

You are my missing piece
I've been searching to find.
Now my life is complete
And forever refined.

RADIANCE OF YOUR SMILE

July 29, 2008

The radiance of your smile
Penetrates my heart,
Refreshes my soul,
And caresses my being
With your comforting love.

It brightens my day,
Lights up my night,
And carries with it
An eternal smile,
Forever imprinted
On my mind.

FAIRYTALE NIGHT

July 29, 2008

We walk hand in hand
By the shore in the night.
You are gazing at me
Under stars shining bright.

And the tickling breeze,
It caresses our souls.
And the moon up above,
Captivates and takes hold.

Our lips lightly brush,
And the sparks fly around,
With the sweetness and magic,
Our hearts now surround.

And we join as one,
On this fairytale night.
We're forever entwined,
By the love burning bright.

And no matter our path,
In this world so divine,
Your love will forever
Imprint on my mind.

NO MEANS OF DREAMS

August 11, 2008

There are no means of dreams
When I'm dreaming about you.
I just let my thoughts flow,
To wherever they go,
And hope that inside them I find you.

There are no means of dreams
When you're there in my mind.
I just let you embrace me,
With your love, interlace me,
And take hold of me from inside.

There are no means of dreams
When you're there in my heart.
I just let you inside me,
To my soul that burns free,
And hope that you never do part.

There are no means of dreams
When you live in my soul.
I just know you will linger,
Wrapped around my finger,
And forever within me you'll glow.

There are no means of dreams
When I think of that day.
I just know it was fate,
That you're here to date,
And that everything will be okay.

There are no means of dreams
When I hunger for you.
I just know I'll be fed,
When I dream in my bed,
And stare at the stars there with you.

There are no means of dreams
When you're my breath of life.
I just live for your presence,
As I drink up your essence,
And know that with you I'm alive.

OBSESSED AND CONSUMED
August 11, 2008

I'm obsessed and consumed...
By the very thought of you,
By your name that rings in my ear,
By the vision of you in my eyes,
By your voice that penetrates my soul.
It is you who I live for,
You who I consume
Every second of every day,
As I breathe in your essence,
The drops of life that you feed me
To keep me afloat
In this ever changing world.

BIT BY BIT TORN APART

August 25, 2008

You said you had a girlfriend.
How did you think I'd feel?
Did you think I would like it?
Did you think I would heal?

I was already shattered,
But the news cracked me more.
And to fly over there,
Now I wasn't so sure.

Didn't think I could stand it
Knowing you are with her;
But I just had to see you,
Had to walk through your door.

So I filled up with courage,
And flew there to see you;
And I went on that tour,
To be closer to you.

But it ended so fast,
Faster than I expected.
And you went on your way,
While I was affected.

I knew you were near,
Yet you seemed far away.
Never once did you call me,
Or write me those days.

It's like I was no longer
That important to you.
It's like you didn't care
About being friends too.

You did not say good-bye,
When you knew I was leaving.
And so I flew back home,
Deep inside of me grieving.

And I wonder why you
Promised we can be friends,
When all that you did,
Was ignore me in the end.

Why you pushed me aside.
Left me there to burn.
Left me crumbling in pieces.
Left my heart being torn.

Why you couldn't just tell me,
To just go on my way,
And forget about friendship,
And forget all those days.

Did you think it was best,
To just not say a word?
That it wouldn't hurt me;
Now that is absurd.

You knew how I felt
For you right from the start,
So you should have known
What was there in my heart.

And you knew very well
I'm an emotional soul,
And that things that are said
Can take their toll.

Yet you just lived your life,
Told me nothing at all,
And you didn't protect me,
Only made me feel small.

I felt I didn't matter,
Not to you or to others,
And I felt there's no reason,
There's no reason to bother.

To hook up with a guy,
Something special to start.
Because then in the end
I'd be left with a heart,

That is torn, that is damaged,
That can only feel pain.
So no reason to suffer
When there's nothing to gain.

So I placed myself there
In the shell all alone,
And I chose to live life
Without guys on my throne.

It was better that way
And I felt it would be,
Just the kind of life
That was meant for me.

THROUGH THE LOOKING GLASS

September 30, 2008

Outside looking in,
On the other side of the ocean,
On the mountain of love,
You are the melody inside my heart,
Burning passion
Exploring me.
A closed bar
Chained to your love,
I'm too blind to notice
You make me feel beautiful.
Stains of red,
The bottle of pain,
My escape
Through the looking glass,
Broken hearted bliss.

A TALE OF LOST LOVE

October 2, 2008

Somewhere far off in the distance,
The little girl huddles near a tree,
Writing another masterpiece.

The air is refreshing,
Her mind is relaxed,
Thoughts flowing weightlessly onto the paper.

The caress of surrounding nature,
Speaks to her mind,
Speaks to her soul.

She sits there weaving a tale of emotion,
A tale of a sweet love turned bitter,
A tale of a love that is lost forever.

Her one true love has vanished,
Vanished from her world to be with another,
As if the love they had shared meant nothing,

Nothing but a fling that came and went,
When in her heart it seemed to be the beginning
Of a love that would never die.

CLOSING YOURSELF TO LOVE

October 3, 2008

You can lock yourself up in a room all alone.
You can sulk over guys that don't sit on your throne.
But you'll only sink deeper in the sea of despair.
And you'll jail yourself from the love in the air.
You will say farewell to love and being happy.
And your life will turn bitter and old and sappy.
So why shut yourself out from the vigorous world,
When somewhere near, love awaits to be swirled.

STROLL DOWN BROADWAY

October 17, 2008

We walk out into the night,
The movie theatre behind us.
The full moon and the endless stars
Beckon us and illuminate the night.

The ferry is our final destination.
And while the subway will speed us there,
Why rush on such a beautiful night
When there's lasting memories to be created?

We turn onto Broadway,
And stroll down until it ends,
Until it merges with the street
That leads to the ferry.

The air is refreshingly pleasant,
Time is at a stand still,
And here we are on Broadway
Walking together, savoring the moment.

And through it all,
We chat about our lives,
About our problems with the rentals,
About other things that connect us together.

We find ourselves on the same frequency,
Realizing we share the same agony,
The same turmoil and frustration
Of being under the rentals' wing.

We realize that we need to escape from their grasp,
From their control of our existence,
And set a path for ourselves,
Where we live and roam solo,

Where we make our lives the way we want to
And not the way they tell us should be.
We cannot let them control us any longer,
And have to set ourselves free,

But we are the only ones who can do that.
We are the only ones who can save us,
The only ones who can release
Ourselves from their grasp.

I start to feel that we're one in the same,
That we're a link in the chain,
That we are meant to be,
And I never want this moment to end.

Standing only inches apart,
I want to keep on walking forever
With you by my side,
And never get to that ferry,

Because the closer we get to the boat,
The closer the end of our time together,
Not just of our stroll down Broadway
But of the relationship that we have.

SWEET LOVE

December 2, 2008

There in the depths of my mind,
You consume me both day and night.
And thinking about you I find,
The widest of smiles in flight.

In moments when sorrow is near,
A thought of you hides it away,
And happiness reigns so dear.
I'm soaring through passing of day.

I feel your presence beside me,
Even though we're oceans apart.
And I crave for your soul to guide me,
To the sweet love that burns in my heart.

FILLED WITH DESIRE

December 26, 2008

It is an awesome treat
To see you light up the screen.
I am filled with desire
To reach out my hands,
And pull you out of the screen,
Right into my embrace,
Into the comfort of my bedroom.

I am filled with desire
To whisper sweet things in your ear,
And to let you know
That in my heart,

You are the magic,
You are the fun,
You are the mystery,
The adventure,
The sun,

You are everything,
I hunger for,
You live in me
Forevermore.

DROWNING (IN MY OWN TEARS)

December 27, 2008

You and I parted for a brief moment.
You were to return to me
But you never did.

And so there I was
Sitting in my room,
Enveloped by sorrow,
Deep and strong.

Tears flew from my eyes
Like raging rivers.
I felt so alone, so empty,
Wishing you back,
But that wasn't to be.

The brief moment dragged on
Like a never-ending song,
And I sat there drowning,
Drowning in my own tears.
They flooded my face, my being,
And the room around me.

I wonder what happened,
What caused you to not return to me,
At the very least to bid me farewell,
And tell me we must part for a short while.
It was not your intention I know.
You'd never leave without a good-bye,
But still I wish it hadn't happened.

You are the best part of my life.
I need you here with me
Now and forever.
I hope you will return to me soon,
And that you haven't vanished from my life
Never to return,
Leaving me here alone
Drowning in my own tears.

TODAY IS THE DAY

January 29, 2009

Seating for two, room for one,
She sits and stares
At the empty chair in front of her.

The glass of wine between her slender fingers
Tastes extremely bitter,
And so do the tears that sting her face.

Only a year ago today,
Was the day when she first tasted love;
Now a year later she tastes the death,
The bitter hollowness of being alone,
Being without the one who lives deep in her soul,
The one for who love burns in her heart.

His presence still roams this world,
But it roams the world of another,
A being that holds no connection,
No resemblance to the soul she is,
To the flesh that hides the spirit
Roaming inside her.

Their relationship was picture perfect.
Everything was exactly as they desired,
Yet there had to be a viral spec,
An invisible molecule that spread itself
Through them, through their existence,
And tore them apart bit by bit.

No one knows how it happened
But today is the day she tasted love and death,
Drank the sweet and the bitter juices.

Today is the day that her love has died
Taking her soul along with it,
And every crumb that lay in her wake.

SPECIAL BOND

January 30, 2009

This special bond
That exists between you and I,
Will never die out,
Will never break,
For you mean too much to me
To ever let you go.
You live deep inside me
And you always will,
For there can be no other way.
I do not see myself
Living here without you.
Where there is me, there is you.
And that's how it will always be
No matter what happens.

DISCARDED LOVE

January 31, 2009

You told me you loved me,
And I thought your feelings mirrored my own.
I must have missed the crack in the glass
Because you vanished from my life,
Without a word, without a warning.

You obviously never loved me;
Yet you spit this lie in my face,
And then discarded me like a piece of junk.

You left me here to wonder why I give in to love
When it always ends in bitter heartache.
You left me here to drown in my own tears;
To bleed from an already broken heart.

SOMETHING THAT WILL NEVER BE

February 26, 2009

I wanted you in my life forever.
I did not care about titles,
About what we were to each other;

All I wanted was for you to be here,
You and I hanging out,
Chatting away about anything,
Or nothing at all.

I just wanted to be in your presence,
Wanted to know I am cared about;
But all that never happened,
And I was left with nothing but a want,
A desire that would never be real.

HOME INSIDE ME

March 17, 2009

You made a home inside me
Never intending to leave,
And I never want you to go
Because you're what keeps me going
In a world I wanted to STOP
A very long time ago.

MESMERIZED

March 17, 2009

I look at your picture in my frame,
Mesmerized by your smile,
By the light in your eyes.
I stand unmoving for what seems like eternity,
Lost in my own little world,
Where it's you and me
Strolling by the ocean side hand in hand,
Under the diamond moon and stars,
With the gentle caress of the wind,
And the drum of the beating waves.
I hear the chirping birds
Calling out to me louder and louder.
I break out of my trance,
Only to realize it's my cell phone.

SMITTEN

March 17, 2009

I've never seen your face,
Never heard your voice,
Just read your e-mail,
And I'm already smitten.

I know it will be a while
Till I get to see your face,
But I already feel
I'll be even more smitten.

So keep on sending your e-mails
My mysterious love,
Keep on leaving your trail
For me to follow.

WAITING FOR A RING

March 19, 2009

I sit on my bed staring at the phone.
Hours drag in this jailed cell,
But all I hear is muted silence.

Here I am chained to the room,
Unable to make my escape,
Pondering the death of the phone.

Whatever the reason,
I am caught in a game of your absence,
Of my lingering thoughts that enslave me here.

Hours drag in this jailed cell
Along with the muted silence,
And then I hear a ring.

BEING YOU

March 19, 2009

Why do you tease me?
Are you trying to please me?
You don't need to tease to please.
You already do, just by being you.

OUR MEETING

March 19, 2009

Across the miles you and I roam -
I in a never-sleeping city,
You in a hibernating suburb.

We only meet when we drift to the skies,
When darkness surrounds,
And the diamond stars light the way.

It may not be enough,
But for now that's all we'll get,
So I cherish every meeting we hold
In the land of adventurous dreams.

TEDDY

March 19, 2009

Before my teddy was just a teddy,
But now teddy is special
Because inside teddy is you,
My crush,
My love,
My special angel.

My teddy will live forever,
Even when I am gone,
And so will you.
You will live forever
I know it.

ANOTHER LIE

March 26, 2009

You swept me away,
Told me you loved me
        Once,
                Twice,
                        Endless times.

I believed every word,
Every sweet thing
        You
                Kept
                        Repeating.

My insides were melting
And in my heart I knew
        I
                Loved
                        You.

But all that you told me,
All that you made me believe
        Was
                A
                        Lie.

There is nothing left inside me now;
All the love I felt within me
Has
Died
Forever.

How can I ever love again?
How can I believe another
I
Love
You?

How will I know it's real?
How will I know it's not
Just
Another
Lie?

IF I COULD

March 30, 2009

If I could get inside your mind
And tell you, you were wrong
For letting me go to be with another;
If I could make you feel the love
That I felt for you, burning inside me;
If I could make you see just how much
I yearned to be with you
Every second of every day;
If I could make a home inside your body
And discover what makes you tick, think, act;
If I could do all these things and more,
I would find a way to bring you back
Into my life, my embrace, my being.
If I could do all these things and more
You'd be mine forever,
And I'd be forever yours.

WILL WE BE TOGETHER?

April 8, 2009

It was fate that brought us together
The first time,
        The second,
                And third.

But it brought us together
In the Virtual World,
And I wonder if, in the Real World,
It can do the same.

Until it happens a part of me
Will feel alone,
        Empty,
                Missing.

If I can't come to you,
Will you come to me?
Can we be together, at last,
In the Real World?

UNNOTICED

April 8, 2009

As I pass you in the hall,
I wave hello with a beaming smile,
And stare into your chocolate eyes,
Hoping you'll come my way;
Yet through it all I remain invisible,
And wonder if you'll ever be mine,
When you're too blind to notice I am even here.

THAT SPECIAL PLACE

April 8, 2009

I want to go to that special place,
Where I feel the passion, the magic, the beauty,
The unison of two emotional souls,
The connection, the spark, the sheer ecstasy.

You're the only one who can take me there,
So accept my invitation
And let us melt into each other
Near the ocean under the stars.

I will bring the blanket,
And all you have to do
Is bring yourself.

MY LOVE FOR YOU

April 8, 2009

My love for you burns like the sun,
Scorching, melting me to the core.
I dissolve in the love,
In all that you are inside and out.

You never leave my mind,
Never leave my heart,
And linger there day and night,
When I'm up, down, and in between.

Constantly in my thoughts,
You live inside me,
And I hope that I
Live inside you too.

OCEANS

April 21, 2009

Another crawling day
By the soothing ocean
Caressing the inner me
Deep to the core; washing away
Every scar imprinted within
From the love turned bitter
Gnawing at my heart.
Here I am in the safety,
In the comfort of this force
Jolting me back to life,
Knowing that with time's passing
Love will bloom once more,
Making me whole again,
Never letting me wither.
Oh how the love will spill its waves,
Penetrating me inch by inch,
Quenching my thirst for beauty
Resting, waiting to unfold.
Spring will open its wings
To the magic, to the love hidden
Under the snowy plains of sleep.
Velour kisses of the sun
Will fill my vacant heart
Xanthic from winter's rotten fruit,
Yanking me to the healing light,
Zenith of life enwrapping me still.

MUSIC FOR MY SOUL

April 22, 2009

Your alluring voice is music for my soul,
Wrapping me with a melody of tears,
Its violin strings pulling my defenses.
I drown in your passionate song,
And surrender to the vibrations
That penetrate every angelic note
That escapes from your luscious lips.

BARE MYSELF

May 12, 2009

I bare myself bit by bit,
Bare the secrets of my soul,
Of my existence in this world.
I feed you every drop
And wonder what you will do.
Will you keep them locked inside?
Or will the whole world
Know everything I revealed?
Meant for only you alone.

WHAT WILL YOU DO?

May 12, 2009

If I tell you *NO*
Will you obey?
Or will you push further?
Force me to do something
I am not ready to do.

Will you wait till I say *YES?*
Or will you leave
And find another,
Who will always obey,
Who will always say *YES*?

LOVE STORM

May 14, 2009

I sail away through stormy seas,
Come crashing down on my knees,
I pray for you to help me please,
To rid me of this love disease.
The boat is small with me inside,
Rocks back and forth on roaring tide.
Will I be saved from deadly ride?
Or will I capsize left to hide,
From love, from all I'll leave behind?
Will you, will others really mind?

NAP TIME

May 19, 2009

He curls up atop his bed
And slowly closes his eyes,
Then drifts into that special place
Where princess roams and magic flies,

Where princess sprinkles in the air
The ever blooming seeds of love,
His heart becomes the sweetest garden
And warmest smiles float above.

When he awakes she'll still be here,
Like stars his face will sparkle then,
And he'll look forward to their meeting
When nap time comes to him again.

YOUR SILHOUETTE MY SECRET GARDEN

May 19, 2009

Whenever I picture your silhouette,
Spring blossoms around me,
Birds sing your beautiful song,
The breeze refreshes my body and soul,
And the endless distance disappears,
Transporting you here to my secret garden
Where bouquets of love spread their wings,
And you and I stroll hand in hand,
Surrounded by this magical moment
Created for just the two of us to savor.

SEE YOU LATER – WHAT DOES IT MEAN?

May 20, 2009

You say *see you later,*
But what does it mean?
Is it hours or days,
Months or years in between?

Or is it *see you never*
So long – farewell;
Don't want you around,
So just go to hell!

You tell me this phrase
That seems simple in meaning,
But to look down deep,
Hard to know where you're leaning.

So tell me the truth,
Do not feed me this lie,
Will I see you again?
Or is this your good-bye?

WAITING FOR HOURS

June 11, 2009

I waited for you
In the blistering cold,
In the settling darkness
Taking its hold;

But you never showed,
Never gave me a sign.
I don't know what to think.
Did you choose to resign?

Or did something else happen?
Why didn't you show?
Please tell me the story.
Which way should I go?

I don't want to stay here
With the rain beating down,
All alone, unprotected,
In my newly bought gown.

I felt like a princess
Set to go to a ball,
But now I feel dirty,
Abandoned, and small.

I don't want to stay here
With night on my side,
Waiting hours for you,
If you chose to hide.

Please give me a sign,
So I know what to do,
I will not waste my time,
Alone, waiting for you.

UNDERGROUND LAIR

June 13, 2009

Slim round tables with a single red rose
Stand inches away from one another.
The lights are dimmed
And classical music floats in the air.

As the notes fly from the stereo,
I see the candle flames dance
In sync to the beautiful melody.

Alone in this underground lair,
We sit lost in each other's eyes,
Frozen, hands interlaced,
Forgetting about the passing of time.

Our moist, hungry lips
Melt into each other,
As you devour me inch by inch.

The more we kiss, the thirstier we get,
So we keep on drinking each other for hours,
An off-the-menu, mouthwatering treat,
That's our appetizer, and more.

It is here, nestled in the underground lair,
Surrounded by the magic of our love,
That we finally become one.

SECTION II
SERENADES OF A CRUSH

LETTING GO

June 16, 2008

I'm letting go of every piece of you inside my heart
I'm letting go of memories that tear me apart
I'm letting go of all I've felt for you right from the start
I'm letting go of thoughts of you that only leave me tart

When it comes to you I am shutting the door
Cause I no longer wish to be fighting this war
It is time to move on to new things up ahead
So when it comes to you all the pieces are dead

I'm letting go of bits of you I've held on to for so long
I'm letting go of letters, of your pictures, and your song
I'm letting go of everything to make myself be strong
I'm letting go of you for good, it's time to move along

When it comes to you I am shutting the door
Cause I no longer wish to be fighting this war
It is time to move on to new things up ahead
So when it comes to you all the pieces are dead

I have suffered so much when you roamed within me
I've shed so many tears that would always fall free
And things only got worse as I sank deep in sorrow
Now it's time for a change, for a brighter tomorrow
I am letting you go so that I can move on
I am starting anew from my life you are gone

When it comes to you I am shutting the door
Cause I no longer wish to be fighting this war
It is time to move on to new things up ahead
So when it comes to you all the pieces are dead

IT SHOULDN'T MATTER

September 5, 2008 & September 9, 2008

It shouldn't matter who we are in name
When we love each other all the same
So why does it matter
Oh why does it matter

When we enjoy
Each other's company
And everything is
The way that it should be

It shouldn't matter what we really are
When we're connected near and far
So why does it matter
Oh why does it matter

When we enjoy
Each other's company
And everything is
The way that it should be

It shouldn't matter that we live apart
When we feel so close from the start
So why does it matter
Oh why does it matter

When we enjoy
Each other's company
And everything is
The way that it should be

Diary of a Crush

Why can't we go on
Without thinking about
The names and the titles
Throw distances out
Why can't we just be
Who we are since the start
And focus on us
And what's inside the heart

What we're in name
And who we are
And that we happen
To live afar
It shouldn't matter
Oh it shouldn't matter

When we enjoy
Each other's company
And everything is
The way that it should be

HERE WAITING FOR YOU

November 7, 2008

Ooo, I'm here for you
And I'll be waiting
Till you come back into my arms and never let me go
Oh, I miss you so

I never wanted to let you go
But I let you slip away somehow
And now
I don't know what to do
Without you

Ooo, I'm here for you
And I'll be waiting
Till you come back into my arms and never let me go
Oh, I miss you so

I wish that you were here right now
I feel so empty and alone
And there
Seems nothing I can do
But wait for you

Ooo, I'm here for you
And I'll be waiting
Till you come back into my arms and never let me go
Oh, I miss you so

Why did I do what I did
Why did I cut you off
From my life
And why am I scared to say
Please come back to me now
Oh I need you

Diary of a Crush

Ooo, I'm here for you
And I'll be waiting
Till you come back into my arms and never let me go
Oh, I miss you so

I miss you
I need you
And I'll be here waiting
But unless I speak up
I miss you
I need you
Won't be enough
To get you back

Still I'll be here for you
And always waiting
Hoping you'll come back into my arms and never let me go
I'll miss you so

Ooooooh
I miss you so
I need you so
I won't let go
You're mine forever

SECRETS ABOUT A BOY

November 10, 2008

She writes in her book
That is hidden away
All the secrets about a boy

And this boy is a boy
That she loves to the core
A boy that lives deep in her soul

She dreamt about this boy at night
Daydreamed about him too that's right
And now this boy's been brought to life
The girl's been saved from all her strife
She's opened up her door
Releasing herself to the world

She writes in her book
That is hidden away
All the secrets about a boy

All the letters they wrote
And adventures they had
All the memories saved in her heart

She dreamt about this boy at night
Daydreamed about him too that's right
And now this boy's been brought to life
The girl's been saved from all her strife
She's opened up her door
Releasing herself to the world

Diary of a Crush

She writes in her book
That is hidden away
All the secrets about a boy

The boy breaking her heart
And just going his way
Though he knew that she loved him to death

She dreams about this boy at night
Daydreams about him too that's right
Wishing the boy back in her life
The girl is drowning in the strife
She's closing her door
Locking herself from the world

The boy the one and only
Who she thought had been the one
And would be her love forever
Is no longer hers and gone
And she weeps there in the silence
Shattered heart and wounded soul
No more boys inside her life now
Dead and broken love's no more

She keeps dreaming about this boy at night
Daydreaming about him too that's right
He was the best thing in her life
But now the cause of present strife
Yet her mind's an open door
To the memories of him and more

ROLLER COASTER LOVE

December 7, 2008

In and out of love
Every time it's tough
Find me in the rough yeah

Don't know how it ends
Parting never friends
Trying to make amends yeah

I'm going through roller coaster love
Up and down, left and right
Will I find myself in love tonight

Always it's the same
Tired of playing this game
Stuck inside the frame yeah

Don't know how to deal
Wish it wasn't real
Some scars never heal yeah

I'm going through roller coaster love
Up and down, left and right
Will I find myself in love tonight

Diary of a Crush

Love is great
But it's complicated
The hurt is there on the side
From it I can never hide
Cause in the end
It's what I get
This hurt inside
I can't forget

I'm going through roller coaster love
Up and down, left and right
Will I find myself in love tonight

WITH EVERY PASSING MOMENT

January 8, 2009 & January 11, 2009

I kiss the rain
I taste the tear
I wonder if
You're really here

You're out of reach
You're out of touch
With every breath
Miss you so much

And so with every passing moment
I wonder if you're gone
I wonder if you vanished from me
Never to return
I cannot live without you
You're the missing piece in me
I need you in my life forever
You have set me free

I touch the window
And stare far
Into the distance
Where you are

Reach out my hand
Find empty space
I'm trapped alone
Inside this place

Diary of a Crush

And so with every passing moment
I wonder if you're gone
I wonder if you vanished from me
Never to return
I cannot live without you
You're the missing piece in me
I need you in my life forever
You have set me free

Do you think of me as I think of you
Do you crave for me as I crave for you
Do you love me as much as I love you now
Do you wish I was right beside you now
In this passing moment
Do you wish we owned it
Just you and me
Just you and me
For all eternity

And so with every passing moment
I wonder if you're gone
I wonder if you vanished from me
Never to return
I cannot live without you
You're the missing piece in me
I need you in my life forever
You have set me free

Are you gone for good
Or are you here
How long will it be
Till you reappear

WHY DO I?

June 26, 2009

I sit by the phone
Waiting for you to call
The hours they pass
With no ringing at all
And I think to myself
Here it goes once more
Caught in this mess again
Falling flat on the floor

Why do I
Always end up in this mess
When everything
Seems to be going right I guess
I must be cursed
Must be my fate to always be
Alone with no one near me
How long am I going to be
A loner here endlessly
I'm tired of this misery
That's haunting me

I sit on the porch
Waiting for you to come
Pick me up for our date
To go party, have fun
But you never show up
Never give me a sign
And I'm caught in this mess
All alone left behind

Diary of a Crush

Why do I
Always end up in this mess
When everything
Seems to be going right I guess
I must be cursed
Must be my fate to always be
Alone with no one near me
How long am I going to be
A loner here endlessly
I'm tired of this misery
That's haunting me

Everything seems to be going just fine
But then why do I find myself left behind
Is there something about me that scares them away
Is it something I do, is it something I say
I just want to be happy, I want to be free
Not from guys but from messes and from misery
And I wonder if that'll ever be

Why do I
Always end up in this mess
When everything
Seems to be going right I guess
I must be cursed
Must be my fate to always be
Alone with no one near me
How long am I going to be
A loner here endlessly
I'm tired of this misery
That's haunting me

YOU COMPLETE ME

July 3, 2009

With every day that goes by
That I don't get to see you I
I find I miss you more and more
And wish you'd walk right through my door

Cause you complete me
Cause you are the light that I see
Living inside of me

With every day that we don't speak
I find my heart a little weak
Until I hear your voice so true
Don't know how I will make it through

Cause you complete me
Cause you are the light that I see
Living inside of me

You are the light that lives in me
With you I always yearn to be
With you I feel alive and free
Oh you complete me

Yeah you complete me
Yeah you are the light that I see
Living inside of me

Diary of a Crush

Yeah you complete me
Yeah you are the light that I see
Living inside of me

Fate brought us together
And together we'll stay
We complete each other
In every way

NEVER PLAYED WITH YOUR HEART

July 28, 2009 & July 31, 2009

It was so easy for you
To let me go out of the blue
Don't understand why you would do
This baby
It's crazy
But maybe
It's better this way

Why do you say that I've
Broken your trust when I've
Been honest from the start
I've never played
Never played with your heart

It was so easy to say
That I stole your dream away
Can't believe that you would think that hey
Oh baby
You're crazy
And maybe
It's good you're on your way

Why do you say that I've
Broken your trust when I've
Been honest from the start
I've never played
Never played with your heart

I'd never take credit for something that I didn't do
So why'd you go on thinking that's something that I would do
I have been true to you right from the start
I can't believe that you want us to part

Diary of a Crush

Why do you say that I've
Broken your trust when I've
Been honest from the start
I've never played
Never played with your heart

SECTION III

FANTASIES OF A CRUSH

YOU AND I IN THE ROSE GARDEN

September 12, 2007

I lie there on the cool grass of a rose garden holding a green apple in my hand. The sun is shining down on me just enough to warm my soul. The birds resting on tree branches are singing away their melodic masterpieces. I call out your name, and it echoes in the air around. I hear your footsteps running and you appear before me in all your glory.

You're as handsome as ever in your khaki shorts, and beige sleeveless t-shirt. You gently caress my hand, and brush your luscious lips against my own, sending tickles through my entire body. Then you take the apple from my hand, take a big bite of it, and with your tongue, let me taste some of that juicy goodness that is dripping onto the grass. We continue our little eating game until there is nothing left of the fruit but seeds.

But that is just the appetizer. Next comes the main course. That's where we playfully rid ourselves of our garments, and with hands interlaced run around the rose garden until we get to our secret little spot. It is there we find our little waterfall cascading into a clear blue pond. We run into the trickling water, our bodies being refreshed by the cool liquid, and then lock ourselves in a tight embrace as we lay our bodies atop the water. Everything around us melts away and our bodies drown in synchronized beat as the birds serenade us with their romantic solos.

YOU AND I AND THE WEEPING WILLOW

September 14, 2007

You and I are walking hand in hand down by the ocean side. I am wearing my blue/orange tankini bathing suit and you've got your blue/orange short tight swimming shorts. The sun has already set, and the moon is slowly peeking in the darkened sky. It's cool and refreshing down by the water with a gentle breeze blowing in. The sandy pathway stretches far and wide, and we journey down that pathway until we reach our weeping willow, the one with our initials engraved inside of a heart.

When we finally get there feeling slightly exhausted from the long stroll, we sit down on the cool grass beneath the hanging tree branches and whisper sweet nothings in each other's ears. In the process we lightly tickle each other's flesh to the point of a quiet whimper. Suddenly our little foreplay leads you to position yourself on top of me, embrace me ever so gently, and rock me to the rhythm of the beating waves and our quickened thumping heartbeats. It's not long before our swimwear is somewhere out of sight and our cool naked bodies are clinging together in a passionate dance of lovemaking that not only flames with colorful fireworks, but an endless sparkle of diamond like stars that appear in the sky overhead. As we melt away in each other, the faint melodic chirp of the hidden birds serenades us into the land of dreams.

YOU AND I AND YOUR BLUE BMW

October 2, 2007

It's around nine in the evening. The dark sky and its surroundings are illuminated by the diamond like stars and the silvery moon that light up the night. I am sitting on my porch steps waiting for your blue BMW to slowly make its way down the hill near my house. All of nature's intriguing beauty takes hold of me, and I drift away dreaming. Within ten minutes or so, your car comes into view but I am still too lost in my dream to notice. Instead of honking you turn off the engine and get out of the car.

As you approach me, you gently brush your lips against mine to say hello and at the same time bring me back to reality. Then you reveal a violet orchid, from its hiding place, behind your back, and place it in my hand; I surround it with my silky fingers. You interlace your fingers with the fingers of my free hand and lead me to your car. You open the door for me to get inside, close it once I am comfortable, and go around to the driver's side to sit down yourself. Then you rev up the engine, turn on your mix trance CD, and we speed down the road and onto the highway. The windows are slightly open, letting the wind play with my hair and caress my face. We drive in silence basking in the moment while melting away with the music. Time seems to stand still.

Finally you drive into the deserted parking lot, put the car to sleep, and open my door so I can step outside. Once again you interlace your hand with mine and we make our way around the corner and down a short flight of stairs underground. There stand small round tables with white tablecloths, a single orchid in a vase, and a candle whose flame is burning bright. Everything is dark except for the glow of the candlelight and hundreds of tiny lamps wrapped around the columns. Classical music is quietly playing from the speakers, and the flame of the candle seems to be swaying along with its melody. We sit down by one of the columns and order two glasses of iced sparkling water and a fruit napoleon to share.

When our order finally arrives, you cut a small bite of the sweet dessert and slowly place the fork into my mouth, and I place a fork in yours. We keep playfully feeding each other until there is nothing left on the plate but crumbs. Then you dab your index finger in those crumbs and let me lick them off your finger. I of course do the same. Now with no sign of the mouth-watering treat in sight, we take sips of the iced sparkling water to refresh ourselves. You then leave a handful of bills on the table and usher me up the stairs to the outside world.

We go around the corner back to your car. We slide into our seats and you turn on your trance music I love so much. For a few seconds we sit there mesmerized, but then you turn to me and taking my face in your hands, brush your luscious lips against mine. At first the kiss is light and gentle, but then filled with yearning, it intensifies and we devour each other with a deepening hunger, our tongues exploring the insides of our mouths. You then position your slim muscular body on top of mine, and still caught in our delicious lip lock, I try to unzip your shorts. It takes a few seconds but I finally get them open. I take out your hidden treasure and stroke it with much pleasure, making you moan. At the same time you fumble with the buttons on my shirt and when you finally get them loose, you caress my nipples and the curves of my breasts causing me to moan as well. Before I have the chance to give you a sign, your treasure finds its way under my skirt and into its throne. You thrust slowly and ever so gently to the rhythm of our quickened heartbeats and the trance music flowing from your CD player. Everything around us melts away and it doesn't even seem like we are in your BMW anymore. We are somewhere in heaven, isolated from the rest of the world. Time stands still and there we are lost in this passionate dance that neither of us wants to come to an end.

YOU AND I AND OUR WINTER WONDERLAND

October 2, 2007

I look out the window and all around me is covered in white. There you are standing below it dressed in a puffy gray jacket and blue hat, scarf, and gloves. You wave at me and call me to come down by throwing a small snowball at my window. I quickly get dressed putting on my white wool coat and red hat, scarf, and gloves, and run down the stairs and out the door into your wide open arms. We stand there embracing each other for a few minutes and then clasping your hand in mine, we skip down the street. The sun is lightly shining in the sky, just enough to warm us, but not melt the snow. Overhead the skies are of a clear light gray, and all around us sparkles like diamonds.

After a bit of skipping, we near the park. When we get to the empty field we begin to roll giant balls of snow to make a snowman. Rolling three balls of different sizes we place one on top of the other. But all's not complete until the snowman is decorated. I remove my hat, place it on top of the snowman, and you wrap your scarf around it, tying a knot. Then we find a few small tree branches, and use them to give the snowman some arms. And to our luck we manage to find a small orange carrot to give the snowman a nose. Once we're done, we admire our creation with huge smiles spreading across our faces.

You take both my hands in yours and brush your lips against mine. In that instant, the chill around me melts away, and I am filled with the warmth of your touch and the electricity that shoots through my entire body. My right leg curls up like that of a fairy tale princess. All of a sudden white flakes start to make their way onto the ground. We part but only for a few seconds so we can remove our jackets and lay them out on the snow. Once we have a place to sit, you gently ease me down onto the blanket we've made, positioning my body into that of an angel. You do the same and clasp your fingers through mine. And as we are showered by all this wet, cold, fluffy goodness, our bodies and lips melt into each other, neither of us feeling the extreme cold that surrounds us. We find ourselves two angels in this winter wonderland that feels just like a fairy tale dream; a dream that neither of us want to come to an end; a dream that will last forever, for we will always be linked together by the magic of snow and by the undying sparkling love that we feel inside our beating hearts.

YOU AND I ON THE MYSTERY MOUNTAIN

February 20, 2008

Being the nature lover that I am, I decide to head up to the mountains. It's a great place to enjoy the beautiful sights around me, to have my troubles melt away, and to have my thoughts roam free. I don't get the chance to head up there often, but when I do, it brings me much excitement, and I always look forward to new hiking adventures, new hidden treasures, and new discoveries.

So on this warm but refreshingly breezy day in May, with the sun shining brightly overhead, I get in my car and with open windows drive up to the mountains up there in upstate NY. I've got classical music coming from the radio as I cruise down the highway with the chirping of the birds floating through my window. The ride usually takes a while but this time it seems very short and I get to my destination in no time at all.

I park the car in my usual spot under the tree, and remove a little shoulder bag from the back seat. It contains a small bottle of water in case I get thirsty during my hike, and my digital camera, which lets me capture wonderful images that I can treasure for a long time to come.

Closing the door behind me I head across the road and onto a winding path that splits into different trails. I usually take the trail that doesn't curve so much, but this time I decide to take the path that is much longer and much more winding. I am already looking forward to hiking up there and uncovering new intriguing things. When I finally reach the end of the trail, I expect to find the place deserted, but when I get to the top I see someone already standing on the exact spot that I wanted to stand and admire the view. The person is facing away from me so I have no idea who it is.

As I get closer I begin to notice short brown hair, and my thoughts drift to you. It seems that I am hallucinating. You are there and I am here and there is no way that you and I could be at the same place at the same time.

Hearing me walking, the person turns around and in that instant my heart skips a bit. It is really you. You are standing before my very eyes on this mystery mountain where I never thought in a million years you'd be found because you are so far across the ocean. How could that be? There is just no way. But there is. You are really here.

We stand there for a brief moment both speechless and very surprised to see each other. It is so unexpected for us both. Once the moment passes, we run to each other and lock ourselves in a tight embrace. After a few minutes, we tear ourselves apart from each other, and interlacing our fingers together, stare out at the vast expanse that spreads around us. The view is so breathtaking, with the lake gently flowing down below, large green mountains spreading in front of us, and the flying birds serenading us with their song.

You turn me toward you and gently brush your lips against mine. As we stand there kissing, little droplets start to trickle from the sky. We don't even notice that rain is coming down until it starts to downpour. Even then we don't run for cover but instead stand their kissing under the spring shower. Our gentle lip lock becomes even more passionate as the rain increases its force and we find ourselves removing each other's clothing until all that's left is our underwear. And then because the mountain is not that high from the ground we hold hands and together dive into the lake. And it is there that we melt into each other as do our surroundings.

What led me to you on this day in May, and how we ended up together on this mountain, is indeed a mystery, but it is our mystery, and one we don't need an explanation for. All that matters is that we are finally together just like we hoped would happen someday in the not too distant future. All that matters is that we can finally share and drink up all the love that we feel for each other that has built up all these years being trapped there in cyberspace unable to get out into the real world.

YOU AND I IN MY BEDROOM

December 17, 2008

I am sitting in my room chatting away with you on the computer. As always, I am enjoying our conversation. Then from the screen of my laptop I see you jump at me and I reach out my arms and grab hold of you. We embrace each other and stay that way for a while without a care in the world. Tears of joy start to fall down our faces. We part and stare deep into each other's eyes. Time comes to a stand still. You brush the strand of hair from my face, your touch making me shiver. You embrace me to warm me up, lightly brushing your lips against mine, never letting me go.

At that moment the room turns dark and the stars on my ceiling light up for a magical moment. We stare at them and together make a wish, sealing that wish with another light kiss. Then we lie atop the smooth sheets and dream together, dream of each other and our deserted island.

I serenade you with my song, and glide my finger down your arm. Then I turn so I am looking down at you, and stare again at your deep intriguing eyes. You stare at mine and we are both lost in a trance. A magnetic force gently pulls us together until there is no space left between us. I whisper things in your ear; only the best compliments in town. My breath tickles your ear, and your neck. Then you move down on the bed and position yourself on top of me whispering things in my ear. We cuddle and sway to the music only we can hear. We then pause for a second to again stare deep into each other's eyes. While lost in this trance, we slowly and playfully rid ourselves of top layers followed by lower layers, and interlace our legs and arms and dance until we go to heaven.

YOU AND I IN THE MAGICAL FOREST

July 25, 2008

It is a beautiful sunny day, and I am hopping through my magical forest. I don't know what it is, but something is dragging me further and further into the dense woods. I am not one for a great sense of direction in the woods, but I keep on going, without ever stumbling to find my way. It's as if I am hypnotized.

Before I know it, the sun is beginning to set and everything around me is getting dark. I have no idea where I am but I can hear what sounds like splashing water. Being the curious cat that I am, I keep on hopping closer to the sound, calling out, "Who is there?". No one answers, but I can see before me a small clear lake with something floating on top of it. As I get closer I realize that it is a slim naked body of a male. His eyes are shut and he seems so still floating atop the water.

Without even thinking about it, I jump into the lake and put my ear to his chest trying to hear if he is breathing; he is not. Then I pick up his frail head, and cradling it in my arms, brush my lips against his with such ferocious passion that I feel electric jolts attack my body. My lips seem to have glued themselves to his because they are locked and my tongue is devouring every inch of his mouth. He doesn't seem to flinch, so I keep on at it for what seems like an eternity, enjoying every drop of his heavenly juice that my lips and tongue get to absorb.

At last he comes to and encircles his arms around me. I don't seem to mind, and let him have a moment of pleasure. Then parting my lips from his, I motion for him to come to shore. He is a bit clumsy for he is still slightly out of it, so I help him out of the water. When I see him standing there in all his glory, all slim, lean, and tall, with delicious chocolate eyes, short spiky hair, and an erect treasure of his, I am mesmerized. It's as if a spell was cast, and I have found *the one*. We stand there for a moment staring at each other, not saying a word. It is the calling of the owl that brings us out of our trance.

"You have saved my life, Princess. Thank you! How can I ever repay you for this kind gesture?" proclaims the male.

"How do you know of my calling? I have not revealed myself to you as yet?" I ask.

"Oh but you have Princess. When your lips met mine and your tongue went inside my mouth, I experienced an electric shock, and an image of your beautiful curvy figure fleshed in my mind. It could only belong to that of a princess," he says.

"Oh my. You are quite something. Unfortunately I know not of your identity, and it's only fair for me to know whom I had the pleasure of bringing back to life, for which of course you must repay me."

"Well, if you insist, you can refer to me as Fin, the lover of the sea. And whatever it is that I must do to repay you for saving my life, I will."

"Ok Fin. Your repayment starts this very moment."

I wrap my arms around him and play with his hair. And then a force pulls us together and our lips meet. We both feel sparks fly around us as our lips entangle, locked in a passionate kiss that keeps getting hungrier and hungrier. Fin picks me up into his arms and carries me into the water and underneath the waterfall. It is there that our bodies unite as one and the magic happens.

It is very dark in the woods now, but the spark between Fin and me illuminates the night. Taking Fin by the hand, I lead him through the darkened woods into my castle. I don't have to know where I am going because whatever led me to that lake is leading me to my throne, and that something, or rather someone, is my one true love Fin.

YOU AND I BY THE OCEAN

July 1, 2009

I walk onto the boardwalk and there you are sitting under the weeping willow, gazing far onto the endless ocean, listening to the beating of the waves against the rocks down below. You are lost in this mesmerizing moment not noticing me standing there calling out your name. It is my light touch against your cheek that brings you back to reality. You say "hello, how nice to see you!" and ask me to join you on the grass. I happily oblige and sit down beside you. You smile at me and I smile back, and we sit there gazing at the ocean, listening to the waves, savoring the moment. Then still staring far into the distance, you take your fingers and interlace them with mine, and I feel electricity run up my arm and shoot through my entire body. I turn to you and you turn to me, and interlacing our other fingers, our lips meet in a light caress and then intensify their game. We sit there under the weeping willow surrounded by the ocean's music, making music of our own with our luscious lips.

ABOUT THE AUTHOR:

Lena Kovadlo was born in Minsk, Belarus on December 24, 1982. She moved to the United States in November 1992 and currently resides in Staten Island, NY.

Writing is her obsessive passion. She has brought to life hundreds of poems and lyrics, and she has also written prose, short stories, fiction, and non-fiction pieces.

With much success in the world of writing, she is proud to be the recipient of **Achievement in Poetry** and **Editor's Choice** awards and be a winner in various writing contests, among which are poetry and lyric contests...

She enjoys writing, reading, singing, dancing, performing, listening to music, surfing the net, cooking, traveling, hiking, sports, and much more...

Her poetry can be found published in poetic anthologies. Besides that, her poetry and other writings are featured on writing.com (where she has her writing portfolio) and on gather.com.

To check out Lena Kovadlo's writing and find out more about her please visit these sites:

- Writing Portfolio: http://www.writing.com/authors/pop4star
- Website: http://lovebuglena.webs.com
- Gather Page: http://lovebuglena.gather.com